To Bromley College,

Best wishes

Oct '14

'What a splendid book! It is a wonderfully clear insight into the minds of those on the autistic spectrum. I found it very helpful and very engaging and will have no hesitation in recommending it to any teacher.'

– Paul Sanders, visiting music teacher, Bromley Youth Music Trust, UK

'Many people with ASDs may not recognise instances of non-literal language and have difficulty in figuring out intended meaning… Michael clearly demonstrates this in an amusing and thought-provoking way in his book and has produced an excellent, invaluable tool to help people with ASD and anyone involved with ASD.'

– Helen Bull, Specialist Advisor for Social & Communication Difficulties for Bromley Education Services, UK

'Michael's pictures are an excellent resource. I use them when I deliver training or write advice for schools as part of my advisory role within a local education authority. I always highlight the use of visual support to aid the understanding of language… I thoroughly recommend them.'

– Jane Rowland, teacher working with students on the autism spectrum, Kent County Council, UK

'The author superbly illustrates (in more ways than one!) the absurdities of the English language. Whilst I'd picked up many of the expressions over the years, his examples enhanced my comprehension and revealed eye-opening autistic interpretations of familiar phrases.'

– Graduate with Asperger's Syndrome (late diagnosis)

'I have used Michael's pictures in training sessions with mainstream staff to show just what it means to have literal understanding. People are amazed and fascinated by the memorable examples he gives... I have found them to be an invaluable and thought-provoking resource.'

— Sue Carter, teacher of pupils on the autism spectrum

'Michael's book is a really useful tool to help young people with ASD make sense of how non-ASD people see the world. It is also invaluable for non-ASD people to understand how confusing – and sometimes scary – our words can be for those who think literally! I highly recommend this book to anyone who works or lives with ASD.'

— Wendy Warne, Family Service Manager, Burgess Autistic Trust, UK

WRITTEN AND ILLUSTRATED BY MICHAEL BARTON

FOREWORD BY DELIA BARTON

IT'S RAINING CATS AND DOGS

AN AUTISM SPECTRUM GUIDE TO THE CONFUSING WORLD
OF IDIOMS, METAPHORS AND EVERYDAY EXPRESSIONS

Jessica Kingsley *Publishers*
London and Philadelphia

First published in 2012
by Jessica Kingsley Publishers
73 Collier Street
London N1 9BE, UK
and
400 Market Street, Suite 400
Philadelphia, PA 19106, USA

www.jkp.com

Library of Congress Cataloging in Publication Data
Barton, Michael.
It's raining cats and dogs : an autism spectrum guide to the confusing world of idioms, metaphors, and everyday expressions / Michael Barton ; foreword, Delia Barton ; illustrator, Michael Barton.
p. cm.
ISBN 978-1-84905-283-2 (alk. paper)
1. Autism spectrum disorders--Patients--Language. 2. Autistic people-- Language. 3. English language--Idioms. 4. Metaphor. I. Title.
RC553.A88.B373 2012
616.85'882--dc23
2011039514

British Library Cataloguing in Publication Data
A CIP catalogue record for this book is available from the British Library

ISBN 978 1 84905 283 2
eISBN 978 0 85700 588 5

Printed and bound in Great Britain

CONTENTS

SHORTENED EXPRESSIONS   37

EVERYDAY EXPRESSIONS AND SAYINGS 41

INSTRUCTIONS AND STATEMENTS 89

FOREWORD

People with high functioning autism or Asperger's Syndrome are usually obsessively logical in their thinking and comprehension of language. However, they often have exceptional memories and thus substantial factual knowledge and extensive vocabularies. This results in people overestimating their ability to understand abstract concepts.

This book was originally conceived when Michael was in junior school. He clearly had difficulty understanding the complexities of our language in respect of idioms, metaphors, colloquialisms and figurative speech. Whereas most of us interpret meaning instinctively, the high functioning autistic brain works by logically analysing and interpreting language in a literal context.

We therefore adopted a strategy of producing a folder in which he would write down confusing phrases, accompanied by a picture of the meaning that first entered his mind. The correct interpretation was then written underneath. This made it easy for him to memorise each individual phrase so that the next time he heard it he could react appropriately.

This approach proved enormously successful in helping him to make sense of the English language and it has also been invaluable for his teachers, family and friends by providing an understanding of how the autistic mind works.

We had lengthy discussions about how to categorise the drawings in this book. Michael's initial response was to list them all in alphabetical order, which is a systematic and logical approach typical of people on the autistic spectrum. However, as one of the aims of this book is to give ordinary people an insight into how people on the spectrum think, we decided to categorise the drawings according to the reason why the expressions cause difficulty.

Thus, this book will help both people on the spectrum and anyone involved with autism to understand the different thought processes that people with autism use to interpret language. This, in turn, will help us to accept them as individuals who are simply different from ourselves, yet who have skills and talents that we can all benefit from.

Delia Barton

INTRODUCTION

This book has been written to help the reader to understand how people on the autistic spectrum think. They approach all situations totally logically and, as the saying goes, they see everything in 'black and white' (I mention this as 'a saying' because I want to make it clear that I'm not at all colour blind!). However, it is the 'grey areas' that can cause confusion. Seeing the world in this way explains why I'm currently studying at university for a degree in Physics. Having a logical mind makes difficult concepts easy to break down and understand – in fact, it is now believed that many famous scientists, for example Newton and Einstein, had autistic traits.

The logical mind of people on the spectrum influences everything about them, including the way that they interpret everyday situations and expressions. The English language is full of idioms and metaphors, which can be difficult for people on the spectrum to understand because they interpret the sayings literally. Take, for example, 'He laughed his head off.' This could be quite disconcerting if taken literally! I remember being told to 'Hang on' when I was younger, and wondering what to hang on to. When visiting the GP I was told to 'Take a seat.' Where was I supposed to take it to?

People on the spectrum can suffer in the real world if other people don't understand how they think. For example, if a teacher tells a boy to 'Pull his socks up' and he literally does just that, the teacher may interpret it as insolence, which will then result in punishment (I know this from experience). However, if the teacher had read this book and realised that the boy was just following their instructions literally, they would recognise that they were at fault for not being explicit enough. I remember someone once told me to 'Wait a minute.' After 60 seconds I started to get impatient and told them that I'd waited for over a minute. Despite me following their instruction to the letter, they thought that I was being extremely rude.

Thinking in context is something that people on the spectrum struggle with, but neurotypical people do intuitively. When my mum told me to 'Draw the curtains' because I was reading in my room in the dark, my response, which was the first logical thought that came into my head, was 'But I don't have a pencil!' My mum's reply was 'Are you pulling my leg?', which didn't help the situation at all!

To help me understand and make sense of these ridiculous expressions (I'm still not sure why my mum wanted me to pull her leg!) I started drawing the mental images that sprang to mind when I heard them. Underneath each drawing I wrote the actual meaning of the expression so that I could understand and remember what each expression meant, and thus what people were trying to tell me when I heard them. After a while I had a substantial folder of these, and this was the first stage in producing my book.

It's not just idioms and metaphors that can have ambiguous meanings. Signs and instructions can also be illogical. A sign I saw recently is shown below:

It's got to be a very small car to disobey this!

Also on GCSE papers I have seen written, 'This page has been deliberately left blank.' How can it possibly be blank if there's writing at the top?

Instructions on public transport can be very bizarre too. On the London Underground passengers are told to 'Let other people off the train first.' How can anyone get on or off until somebody disobeys this instruction first? People at my local train station are told 'For their safety, passengers are requested to remain behind the yellow line at all times.' The yellow line stretches the whole length of the platform, so how can anyone get on or off the train unless they ignore this instruction? On a bus recently I saw the sign:

SAFETY NOTICE:

Passengers are asked to

remain seated at all times

How on earth were they meant to get off? Were they doomed to be trapped on the bus for eternity?

The only times people speak to me in a clear and concise way are a) during Maths and Physics lectures, and b) when I travel to a foreign country. I'm good at learning languages because of my ability to learn facts easily, which means I have a large vocabulary. And because I'm a foreigner, people speak very clearly and don't expect me to understand any idioms, metaphors or confusing phrases. Also, if I'm sometimes rather blunt or tactless in my response, they assume it's due to my imperfect language skills (rather than my Asperger's) and as a result I get treated as a complete equal, rather than being ignored or ostracised, as so often happens in the UK. Perhaps teachers could better deal with pupils on the spectrum by pretending they are from a foreign country?

Knowledge of how people on the autistic spectrum think is fundamental to accepting and understanding them. I hope that this book will prove useful for both young people on the spectrum who need to learn the true meanings of the various idioms and metaphors within it, and any adults who need to deal with people on the spectrum on a daily basis, and would therefore benefit from gaining an insight into their thought processes.

Michael Barton

CLASSIC IDIOMS

These are phrases or expressions whose sense cannot be derived from the meaning of the individual words. Neurotypical people learn expressions in the same way they learn words. When they hear 'It's raining cats and dogs,' their brain simply recalls that this phrase means 'It's raining really hard.'

My brain logically examines each individual word and then tries to make sense of the resultant sentence. When this approach doesn't work, I have found that drawing a picture enables me to recall the mental image when I hear that phrase, and this helps me remember the true meaning.

It's raining cats and dogs

It's raining really hard

Getting the sack

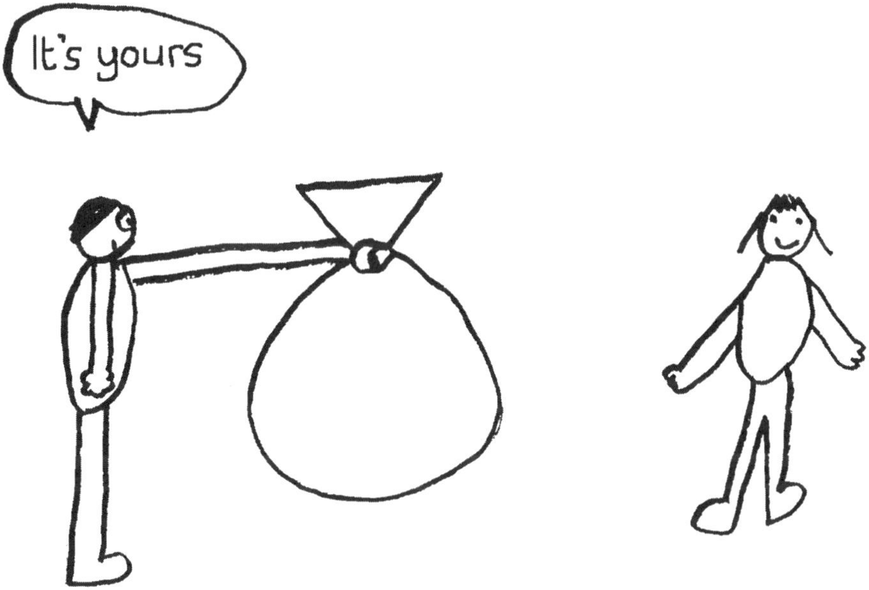

Losing your job

You're pulling my leg!

You're joking!

He went bananas

He went crazy

To chicken out

To not do something
because you're scared

A different kettle of fish

A totally different matter

Stick to your guns

Once you decide to
do something, do it

Feeling under the weather

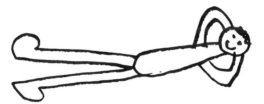

Feeling unwell

I was over the moon

I was very pleased

It's a piece of cake

It's really easy

You're burning the candle at both ends

You're getting up early and going to bed late

It cost him an arm and a leg

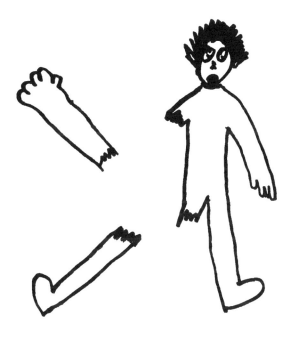

It was very expensive

Your ears are burning!

Someone's talking about you!

He's got something up his sleeve

He has a secret plan or idea

Call a spade a spade

Speak plainly

Going round the houses

Taking a long time
to explain something

Breaking the ice

Helping people feel at ease in a social situation

In a pickle

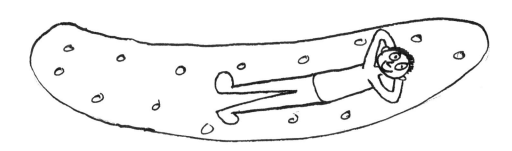

In a tricky situation

He's got the wrong end of the stick

He's got the wrong idea

SHORTENED EXPRESSIONS

In shortened (or truncated) expressions part of the phrase has been left out. For example, 'Put the kettle on' is short for 'Put the kettle on the stove.' 'I feel like a pizza' is short for 'I feel like eating a pizza.' Neurotypicals have simply memorised the phrase and don't even think about whether anything is missing or not.

My brain constructs meaning from the individual words, so 'I feel like a pizza' is literally processed as such. When I hear 'Put the kettle on,' I assume it is the same as 'Put the hat on,' so the kettle must go on my head.

He had the sun in his eye

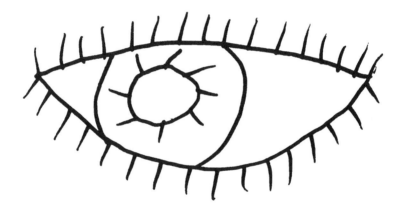

He had the sun shining into his eye

Put the kettle on

Switch the kettle on

I feel like a pizza

I feel like eating a pizza

EVERYDAY EXPRESSIONS AND SAYINGS

Neurotypical people say these expressions without thinking how illogical they actually are. They grow up hearing them on a regular basis and learn them like words.

People on the spectrum need to be explicitly taught what they mean – they do not intuitively recognise that they are idioms. The default response to hearing an idiom is always to assume that the logical explanation is correct. It is extremely confusing when you hear sayings that have nothing to do with what they actually mean.

He's driving me up the wall

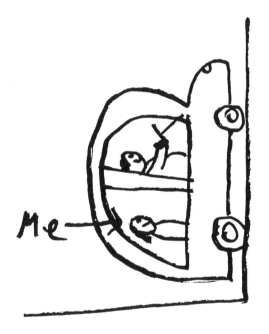

Me

He's making me really cross

His head is in the clouds

He's daydreaming

I've got some time on my hands

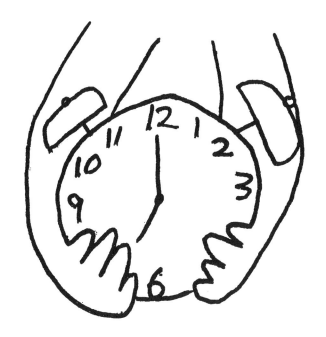

I've got some spare time

It's hard to get your head around it

It's hard to understand it

To cry your eyes out

To cry a lot

A square meal

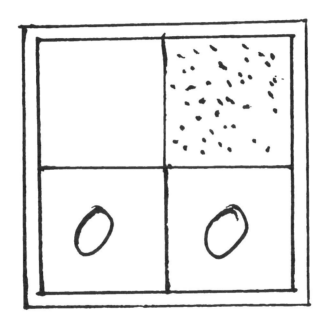

A balanced meal

He has a sweet tooth

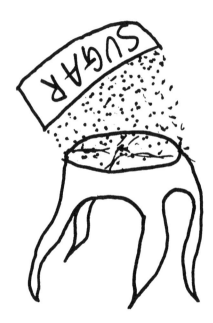

He likes sweet food

A square meal

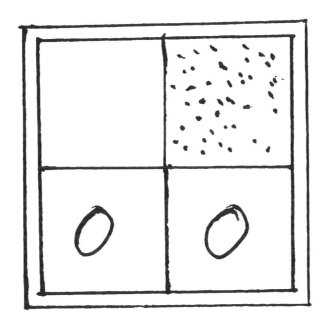

A balanced meal

He has a sweet tooth

He likes sweet food

He gave me a piece of his mind

He was angry and he told me what he thought

My head was spinning

I had many thoughts

I laughed my head off

I laughed a lot

To have a face like thunder

To have a very angry expression

I worked my socks off

I worked really hard

It's not my cup of tea

It's not the kind of
thing I like doing

We didn't meet eye to eye

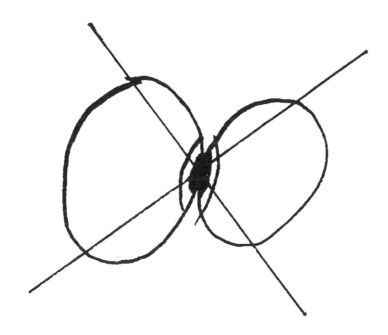

We didn't agree

He is all ears

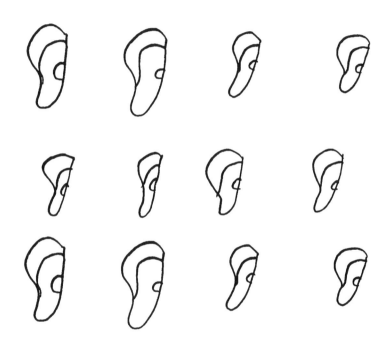

He is paying full attention

To bend over backwards

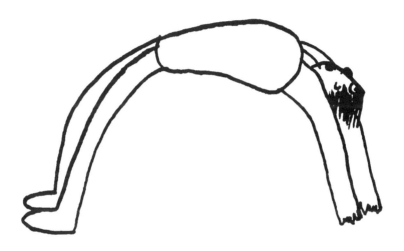

To put a lot of effort into something to please someone

That's how the cookie crumbles

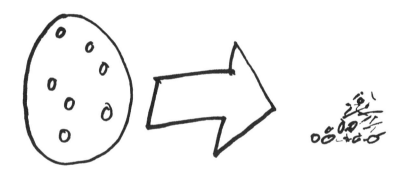

That's just the way things happen

To grab the bull by the horns

To take control of the situation

I changed my mind

I changed my opinion

He went out with a bang

He did something memorable before he left

DOUBLE MEANINGS

If I 'draw' the curtains, am I drawing a picture with a pencil or pulling them together? The neurotypical brain considers the context when it hears this phrase, evaluates the alternative meanings and then comes to a conclusion as to the most likely explanation.

My brain assumes that the first explanation it thinks of is the correct one. So 'draw' usually means 'use a pencil' and, as this is the most likely meaning, I then proceed on that basis. It doesn't even occur to me at the time to consider whether there might be an alternative explanation.

The drinks are on the house!

The drinks are free!

He caught my eye

He got my attention

Catch the bus

Go by bus

You're fired!

You've lost your job

Draw the curtains

Open the curtains

Bear with me

Please be patient

Toast the bride

Drink to the bride's good health

METAPHORS

These are imaginative ways of describing something by likening it to something else; in other words, to help clarify what is being said. For example, 'He flew up the stairs' means 'He went up the stairs really quickly.'

My brain doesn't realise that something is being likened to something else and just takes what is being said literally, so I imagine someone with wings actually flying. So, whereas neurotypicals will use metaphors to aid clarification in sayings such as 'He hit the nail on the head,' they have the opposite effect on me.

I find it almost impossible to remember phrases that don't make sense but I *can* remember a picture or drawing, so using these drawings helps me understand idioms and metaphors in everyday use.

You've hit the nail on the head

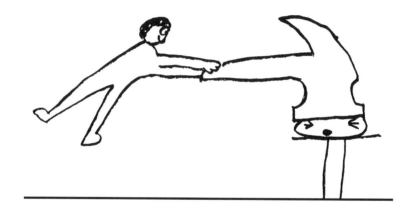

You've got it exactly right

You're winding me up

You're annoying me

He flew up the stairs

He rushed up the stairs

He had egg on his face

He did something to make himself look silly

The bread and butter

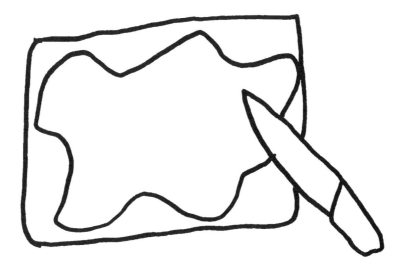

The essentials

Splitting hairs

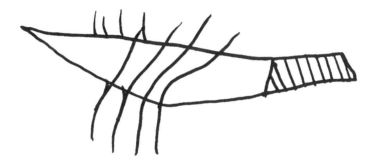

Being very precise

You took the words right
out of my mouth

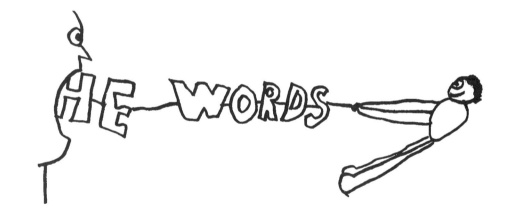

You said what I
was going to say

It's pouring down

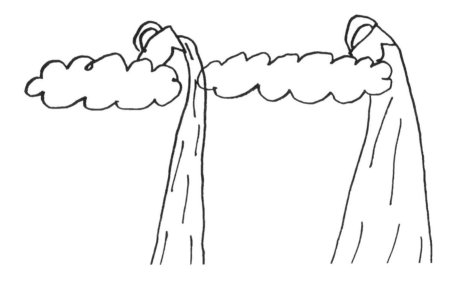

It's raining really hard

I was like a dog with two tails

I was really happy

Put yourself in my shoes

Try to look at things
from my point of view

To be under somebody's thumb

To always do what somebody says

The ball's in your court

It's your turn to do something

He knows it inside out

He knows it very well

He ran around like
a headless chicken

He had no control
over the situation

Keep your eyes peeled

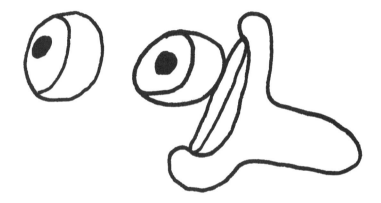

Look out very carefully

To open a can of worms

To do something that will cause future problems

Set the cat among the pigeons

Disturb a peaceful situation

INSTRUCTIONS AND STATEMENTS

People on the autistic spectrum tend to leap straight to the most logical interpretation of an instruction or statement, even if it doesn't make any sense, whereas neurotypical people remember the meaning that is relevant to the situation.

When the teacher told me to 'Pull my socks up' and I did so, I was told off for being rude and cheeky, yet I'd done nothing wrong! (At least, I'd done nothing *deliberately* wrong.) I've also had problems at school with 'Belt up,' 'Wipe that grin off your face' and 'You'd better sharpen your pencil.' So how do I remember these for next time? Easy – draw a picture of them.

Take a seat

Sit down

Hang on!

Wait!

Don't rub it in

Don't keep going on about it

Keep your eye on it

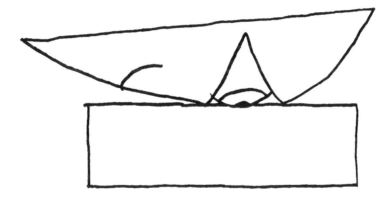

Pay a lot of attention to it

To put your foot down

To say enough's enough

Cut it out!

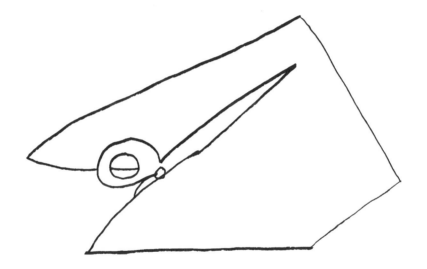

Stop it!

of related interest

Freaks, Geeks and Asperger Syndrome
A User Guide to Adolescence
Luke Jackson
Foreword by Tony Attwood
ISBN 978 1 84310 098 0

Kevin Thinks
...about Outer Space, Confusing Expressions and the Perfectly Logical World of Asperger Syndrome
Gail Watts
ISBN 978 1 84905 292 4

Flying to See Janet
A Fun Guide to the Airport Experience
Laura Vickers
Illustrated by Peggy Wargelin
ISBN 978 1 84905 913 8

Raising Martians - from Crash-landing to Leaving Home
How to Help a Child with Asperger Syndrome or High-functioning Autism
Joshua Muggleton
Foreword by Tony Attwood
ISBN 978 1 84905 002 9

Autistic Planet
Jennifer Elder
Illustrated by Marc Thomas and Jennifer Elder
ISBN 978 1 84310 842 9

The Lovable Liam Series
Jane Whelen Banks
ISBN 978 1 84310 907 5